KU-647-444

ANIMALS UNDER THREAT

ALLIGATOR

SAVED FROM EXTINCTION!

Richard Spilsbury

Heinemann
LIBRARY

H www.heinemann.co.uk/library
Visit our website to find out more information about **Heinemann Library** books.

To order:
☎ Phone 44 (0) 1865 888066
🖹 Send a fax to 44 (0) 1865 314091
💻 Visit the Heinemann Bookshop at www.heinemann.co.uk/library to browse our catalogue and order online.

First published in Great Britain by Heinemann Library, Halley Court, Jordan Hill, Oxford OX2 8EJ, part of Harcourt Education. Heinemann is a registered trademark of Harcourt Education Ltd.

© Harcourt Education Ltd 2004
The moral right of the proprietor has been asserted.

All rights reserved. No part of this publication may be reproduced, stored in a retrieval system, or transmitted in any form or by any means, electronic, mechanical, photocopying, recording, or otherwise, without either the prior written permission of the Publishers or a licence permitting restricted copying in the United Kingdom issued by the Copyright Licensing Agency Ltd, 90 Tottenham Court Road, London W1T 4LP (www.cla.co.uk).

Editorial: Emma Lynch, Jilly Attwood and Claire Throp
Design: Jo Hinton-Malivoire and Tokay, Bicester, UK (www.tokay.co.uk)
Picture Research: Rosie Garai and Liz Eddison
Production: Séverine Ribierre

Originated by Ambassador Litho Ltd
Printed in China by WKT Company Limited

ISBN 0 431 18892 0
08 07 06 05 04
10 9 8 7 6 5 4 3 2 1

British Library Cataloguing in Publication Data
Spilsbury, Richard
Alligator - (Animals under threat)
597.9'84
A full catalogue record for this book is available from the British Library.

Acknowledgements
The Publishers would like to thank the following for permission to reproduce photographs: Ardea pp. **10** (Mary Clay), **16** (François Gohier), **34** , **37** (John Daniels), **41** (Chris Martin Bahr); Bruce Coleman Inc p. **23** (Stephen Kline); Corbis pp. **4** (Hugh Clark), **5** (Farrell Grehan), **7** (Kevin Fleming), **8**, **28** (Raymond Gehman), **13** (Joe McDonald), **22** (Alan Schein Photography), **24**, **29**, **31**, **36** (Philip Gould), **30** (Jonathan Blair), **38** (Kevin Schafter), **39** (Michael T. Sedam); Corbis/FLPA p. **12** (Fritz Polking); FLPA pp. **17**, **26**, **35**, **40** (David Hosking) **20** (T. Davidson); Getty Images p. **11** (Stephen Cooper), pp. **9**, **25**; NHPA pp. **27** (Martin Wendler), **32** (Trevor McDonald), **43** (Joe Blossom); OSF **15**, **33** (Brian Kennedy), **18** (Edward Robinson), **21** (Stan Osilinski); SPL p. **19** (Treat Davidson); Tudor Photography p. **42**.

Cover photograph reproduced with permission of OSF/Bob Bennett.

The publishers would like to thank Dr Chris Tydeman, Environmental Consultant, for his assistance in the preparation of this book.

Disclaimer
All the Internet addresses (URLs) given in this book were valid at the time of going to press. However, due to the dynamic nature of the Internet, some addresses may have changed, or sites may have ceased to exist since publication. While the author and publishers regret any inconvenience this may cause readers, no responsibility for any such changes can be accepted by either the author or the publishers.

Every effort has been made to contact copyright holders of any material reproduced in this book. Any omissions will be rectified in subsequent printings if notice is given to the publishers.

The paper used to print this book comes from sustainable resources.

Contents

Words printed in the text in bold, **like this**, are explained in the Glossary.

The American alligator

The American alligator, *Alligator mississippiensis*, is the only **species** of alligator that lives in the USA. All alligators are members of the **order** of crocodilians, which also includes the crocodile and gharial families. Crocodilians are just one order of **reptiles**; the other familiar groups are snakes, lizards and turtles. All crocodilians look similar: they have enormous jaws full of teeth, a long tail, short legs and a scaly, armoured body, but they are all slightly different on the outside, for example in head shape.

Alligator facts

Of the 23 species of crocodilian, eight are in the alligator family and six of those are called caimans!

The name alligator comes from the Spanish words 'el lagarto', which mean 'the lizard'. It was first used by early Spanish explorers in the Americas.

Telling alligators from crocodiles

Alligators have broader, shorter snouts than crocodiles. They look black when wet and dark grey when dry, whereas crocodiles are typically greenish or tan. However, these differences are not always obvious unless you happen to have a crocodile and an alligator next to each other to compare! The clearest difference is in the arrangement of their teeth (see caption below).

▲ *When an alligator closes its mouth, the fourth tooth from the tip of its lower jaw fits into a socket in the upper jaw so you cannot see it. When a crocodile closes its mouth, the fourth tooth can always be seen (see the picture on page 38).*

Alligators in trouble

About 30 years ago the American alligator was an **endangered** species. When a species is endangered, usually many more individuals are dying than being born. When numbers are dropping this fast, the species is at risk of becoming **extinct**. Alligators were endangered because people hunted and crowded them out from the wild places where they live. This could have meant that there would be no more American alligators left on Earth.

However, American alligators survived and they are now thriving. They are no longer endangered. This is because people decided to protect them. This book looks at alligators, how they live and how they were threatened in the past. It also looks at why and how people changed their attitudes to alligators, and learnt to live alongside them.

American alligators of today are quite similar to their ancestors from the age of dinosaurs.

Crocodilian ancestors

The crocodilians of today are **descendants** of animals that lived around 200 million years ago. We know this because **fossil** skeletons of these animals are very similar to modern crocodilian skeletons. However, some crocodilians, which are now extinct, were rather different. Some types had hooves, while others were very big. Deinosuchus, which lived around 80 million years ago, was up to 15 metres long, more than twice the length of the largest American alligators of today!

Alligator country

Wild American alligators live only in the south-eastern states of the USA. They are a common sight throughout Florida and Louisiana, and most of southern Georgia, Alabama and Mississippi. American alligators live as far west as Texas and as far east as coastal North Carolina. They live in these parts of the USA because of the **climate** and **habitat** there.

The importance of temperature

American alligators live in areas with a **subtropical** climate. A subtropical climate generally has hot, humid summers with lots of rain, and usually mild but sometimes cold winters.

Alligators are **cold-blooded**. This means that their bodies are usually the same temperature as their surroundings. To control their temperature through the day, they have to move around between warm and cooler places. For example, if it is cold, they have to warm up their bodies in the Sun before they can become active.

Warm-blooded animals

Mammals stay the same temperature inside whatever the temperature outside. They are described as warm-blooded animals. However, they generally need to eat more food, more often than cold-blooded animals, in order to give them enough energy to stay warm.

Alligators live along the coasts of the warmest US states (in yellow on the map).

Alligator habitat

UNITED STATES OF AMERICA

N

North Carolina
Arkansas
Alabama
South Carolina
Texas
Georgia
Florida
Louisiana   Mississippi

Man-made wetlands

Alligators are not particularly fussy about what type of wetland they live in. They are usually found in natural wetlands, such as swamps, but they will also live in man-made ones. Alligators are often found in drainage canals, storm drains, swimming pools or pools on golf courses.

The right habitat

American alligators only live within certain habitats in the tropical states of the USA. They mostly live in freshwater **wetland** habitats. Wetlands are the crossover places between land and water. Although these low-lying areas usually contain water for at least part of the year, wetlands may dry out completely, especially in times of **drought**. Examples of typical alligator wetland habitat are the **Everglades** in Florida and the Louisiana bayous. These are both **swampy** areas that vary from areas of slow-moving streams and rivers, to marshy grassland and swamp cypress forest. Both areas provide the right mix of open waterways that alligators can move through, enough shelter, places to nest in and materials to nest with, and plenty of **prey**.

Typical alligator habitats are warm wetlands such as swamps.

American alligators are occasionally found in seawater, or in a mixture of freshwater and saltwater around river **estuaries** and coastal **mangrove** swamps. Although they can live in saltwater for short periods of time, alligators cannot get rid of the excess salt they drink. This is bad for them over long periods. Crocodiles, on the other hand, have special **glands** around their tongues that secrete (get rid of) excess salt.

It is difficult to say exactly how many American alligators there are, because counting animals in the wild is not easy. Sometimes it is tricky because they look similar and might be counted twice. Sometimes it is made more difficult because they move around, or hide in large areas of **habitat**. Nearly all populations of wild animals are estimated. The usual way to estimate is to count accurately the number of animals in a small area of habitat, and then multiply that number by the overall area of that habitat.

Counting alligators

Alligators are most active at night, when it is obviously more difficult for people to see them. One of the most common ways of counting alligators is to follow **survey routes** along waterways where they might be living, in a quiet boat. Observers shine torches at the water's surface. Alligators' eyes generally stick up above the water as they swim along. If the beam of torchlight hits their **retinas**, the light is reflected back, making their eyes shine red.

The number of pairs of red dots seen is the number of alligators present at the water's surface. Although most alligators in an area will be out of sight, this number is assumed to be representative of the total number of alligators in an area. If the survey is repeated enough times along the same route, an average population can be estimated for that route, and then for the whole of the alligator habitat.

During alligator counts, scientists often catch alligators so they can record their age, size and sex.

▶ This engraving shows alligators being shot in the Mississippi *swamps*.

Other ways to estimate population size

People count alligators in other ways too. In areas without too much tall plant cover, people count alligators from planes. This is an effective way to cover a wide area. Another way to estimate population size is to carry out a survey of nests. People count alligator nests on foot, by boat or by air. Each **breeding** female makes one nest, and scientists know that breeding females make up around one third of the total alligator population. So, if there are ten nests in an area, scientists can estimate that the total population size is 30.

By putting together results from many local and state-wide population surveys, scientists estimate that there are around 5 million American alligators in the USA. Between 1 and 2 million of these live in Florida alone.

In the past

People think that there are far fewer American alligators today than there were in the past. During the late 1770s, an American naturalist called William Bartram wrote that in one river, 'alligators are in such incredible numbers and so close together from shore to shore that it would have been easy to have walked across on their heads had the animals been harmless'. Few wild places today are teeming with alligators in these numbers!

The body of an alligator

Alligators have strong, tough bodies to help them survive. The biggest alligators can weigh over 400 kilograms. Most of this weight is muscle and skin.

Armour plating

The body of an alligator, like that of all **reptiles**, is coated in **scales**. These are thick, waterproof pieces of hard skin. Alligator scales are called **scutes**. The scutes on the top of an alligator's body are incredibly tough, because they are strengthened with grains of bone called osteoderms. They form a kind of armour plating that protects the soft body inside. The scales on an alligator's stomach are softer and more flexible, because they have fewer osteoderms.

The thickest and biggest scutes on an American alligator's body run in lines from the neck down to the point of the tail.

Jaws

The American alligator is a carnivore, an animal that eats other animals. It catches **prey** in its jaws. It has 70–80 sharp teeth. If a tooth becomes damaged or worn down, another will grow to replace it. Thick muscles around the alligator's skull can close the jaws together with enough power to crush a deer skull or a hard turtle shell. Remarkably, the muscles used to open the jaws are much weaker. The jaws of a 2 metre-long alligator could be held together by a thick rubber band.

Getting around

An alligator's tail is almost half of its total length. It is flattened from side to side. The alligator uses its tail to swim, by waving it from side to side. When swimming, alligators usually tuck their short legs into their sides to create a more **streamlined** shape. When floating, they stretch out the webbed toes on their back feet to form broad paddles. They use these to remain still in the water.

American alligators can swim as fast as 40 kilometres per hour.

Alligators usually move quite slowly on land. They walk on their stretched legs, with their tail dragging along the ground, and take frequent rests. However, alligators can run like this for short distances. If moving on slippery mud they often slide along on their fronts, pushing with their folded legs.

Under water

Alligators breathe in through their nostrils and mouth. When an alligator dives underwater, skin flaps seal off its nostrils and throat, to stop water getting into its lungs. With the throat flap closed, it can open its mouth under water to catch prey without drowning. Alligators also have flaps that seal up their ears, and a transparent third eyelid that moves sideways across their eyes to protect them from damage under water.

Alligators generally hold their breath for up to 30 minutes when swimming. The air in their lungs makes them float to the surface, so most alligators, especially young ones, swallow stones that stay in their stomach to weigh them down. The stones also help alligators to digest their food.

Keeping the right temperature

Remaining at the right temperature is critical to American alligators, as it is to other animals. If they get too cold or too hot, important changes happen.

Alligators begin to lose their appetite below 27 °C. The **enzymes** in their stomach can only **digest** food above this temperature. If it is colder than this, the food rots. They stop feeding altogether if the temperature is between 20 °C and 23 °C. An alligator grows more slowly if it is too cold. Its body is also less able to fight infections and heal wounds. If alligators get too hot, above 40 °C, they risk heat damage to their skin and internal **organs**.

Hot or cold, male or female

Whether an egg will hatch into a male or a female alligator is decided by temperature. If a newly laid egg is **incubated** at 28–31 °C, the **embryo** develops into a female. Males develop if the temperature is warmer, around 32 °C. Different sexes can be produced in the same nest depending on the egg's location within the nest. The weather and where the nest is made will also have an effect.

Heat-seeking behaviour

Alligators usually stay at 28–35 °C by moving between warmer and cooler places. They move to hot places to soak up heat if they are too cold. This is called **basking**. The skin just below the raised **scutes** on an alligator's back is full of blood vessels. These carry blood warmed by the Sun around the body, raising the animal's internal temperature.

▶ Basking is a vital part of alligator life. Alligators sometimes bask in groups.

During spring and summer, alligators generally bask in the morning and early evening, on riverbanks or in shallow water. In the hottest part of the day, especially during summer, they prevent overheating by staying in the water or in shade. Alligators also cool down by gaping. This is when they open their mouths wide to cool the blood in the vessels just under the skin of their large tongues.

When alligators are under water, they can still breathe because their nostrils are on top of their snout, so remain out of the water.

Surviving cold weather

American alligators become less active and stop feeding as autumn sets in. They dig out dens in muddy riverbanks, using their tails. Dens are burrows with a higher chamber at the end, partly filled with water. In the coldest places, dens can be up to 20 metres long. The water in a den remains at a constant low temperature, whereas the water and air outside may vary from quite cold to freezing. An alligator becomes dormant (it slows down its breathing and other body functions) in its den during winter. It will sometimes emerge on a warmer day. Alligators can easily last from October to March without feeding. They use energy stored in their fat and muscles.

The icing response

Occasionally temperatures drop so low that alligators are trapped below ice. They usually keep their nostrils above the water, but their breathing slows right down. There may be several hours between each breath.

A supreme hunter

Apex predators and other animals

Apex predators, such as alligators, greatly influence the other living things in their **habitat**. For example, muskrats can eat so many marsh plants that there are not enough left for some birds to nest in. So, when alligators eat muskrats, they help both marsh plants and birds.

Most **predators** take the easiest option to get a meal. If an alligator has to choose between an old muskrat that swims slowly and a fit one that can move fast, it will take the slower one. By killing the weakest individuals, alligators improve the chances of fitter muskrats surviving and producing healthy young, so improving the general health of the muskrat population.

Adult American alligators are **apex predators** in the US **wetlands**. This means they are at the top of the food web, no other wild animals catch and eat them. Alligators, however, will eat just about anything they can catch.

Changing diet

When they first hatch from their eggs, young alligators mostly feed on insects, crabs and crayfish, snails and small fish. As they get bigger they eat larger food. Adult alligators mostly eat turtles, racoons, muskrats, large fish, such as gar, and **reptiles** including smaller alligators. Less common foods are **waterfowl**, deer, **livestock**, carrion (dead animals), pet dogs and even people. Alligators also swallow things in the water that are not food, such as bottles, cans and fishing tackle.

This simple wetland food web shows some of the animals American alligators eat at different stages of their life. Alligators only risk being eaten by birds and larger alligators when they are young.

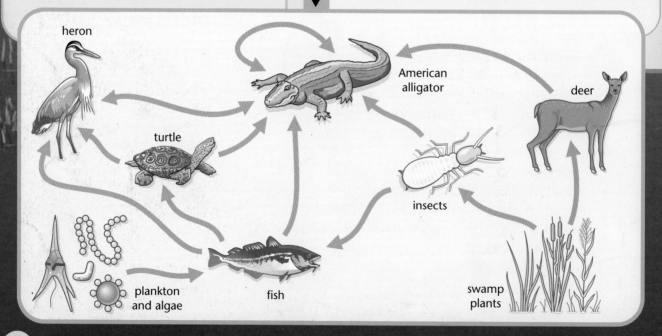

heron

American alligator

deer

turtle

insects

plankton and algae

fish

swamp plants

American alligators often ambush animals or birds, like this pelican, that come to the water's edge to drink.

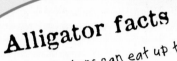

Alligator facts

Adult alligators can eat up to 200 kilograms of food per week, but can go months without food. They usually eat once every 3 or 4 days.

Ways of hunting

Alligators mostly try to ambush **prey** at the water's surface or on shore. Their small eyes, ears and nostrils are raised on their heads so they can stick out when the rest of their body is hidden under water. Alligators have particularly good vision in low light. Their **retinas** have a reflective coating so they can use any available light, even moonlight, to see with. Alligators cannot see so well under water.

Dealing with food

Alligators swallow small prey whole. They kill larger prey by gripping it in their teeth and drowning it. An alligator has no cutting teeth, so it rips chunks off large kills by gripping and then shaking its head. When it swallows food, the large flap in its throat has to open. This is why alligators never eat under water.

It takes longer for large chunks of food to be **digested** than smaller chunks. Alligators have no chewing teeth to speed up the process. Instead they use their gizzard, a small chamber next to their stomach that contains strong acid and swallowed stones. The acid and stones help to break down the food into smaller pieces, before it moves into the stomach.

Gator holes

In the hottest summer weather, the parts of **wetlands** with the shallowest water dry up. This is an even bigger problem during **droughts**. It means there are fewer places for American alligators to cool down or catch **aquatic prey**.

To make sure they always have a cool pool available, alligators create their own. They use their jaws and claws to uproot marsh plants, such as ferns and sawgrass, to clear out a space. Then, shoving with their body and slashing their powerful tail, they dig a pit, piling the mud and plants around its edge. This pit is often called a gator hole.

As the water in gator holes is deep, it takes longer to dry up than shallower stretches of water.

Spotting a gator hole

Gator holes are usually built in the same places in wetlands, year after year. They are often above areas of **bedrock**, which act a bit like a pond lining to stop the water draining away. The mud the alligators dig out when enlarging these holes is rich in **nutrients**. Some plants grow very well in these clear areas of mud, creating patches of plants that are tell-tale signs of a gator hole. Plants such as pickerel weed and red bay grow well on the edges of gator holes. In the deeper water just inside the hole, other plants emerge. One large-leafed plant with small purple flowers is typical of gator holes. It is called alligator flag!

Earth moving

The changes alligators make to wetlands can be impressive. The largest gator holes, usually created by the largest alligators, can be 10 metres across and several metres deep. Apart from gator holes, alligators also create and maintain open water channels. They remove water plants from the edges and dig mud away from the banks. Alligators do this so they can move easily between different parts of their **habitat** to find food, shelter and other alligators, when it is time to **breed**.

The importance of gator holes

These changes are important for other animals in the habitat too. Water in gator holes provides a refuge for animals that might die during dry weather such as fish, crayfish and turtles. Some of these animals become prey for alligators and other **predators**, such as egrets and herons, but many survive until more rains come. When the waters rise, they can spread into other parts of the habitat, along water channels maintained by the alligators. The raised land around the water-filled gator holes becomes an island. Over time this becomes fringed in taller plants that shelter different animals. Gator holes in saltwater wetlands provide rare chances for animals, such as deer, to drink freshwater.

Mud and rotting plants piled up around gator holes provide nest sites for turtles such as the Florida red-bellied turtle.

Territory and breeding

An American alligator normally lives in one area of its **habitat**, called its **home range**. This provides all its food, shelter and water. Females usually have small ranges, around one square kilometre. Males have bigger ranges, over three square kilometres.

A male's home range may include the ranges of several females. For most of the year, alligator ranges may overlap. However, during the alligator **breeding season** in April and May, a home range becomes a **territory**. A territory is an area that is defended by just one animal. The alligator keeps other animals out because the area contains something it wants to keep for itself. For example, female alligators chase away other females to be sure of getting the best nest sites.

Alligators show others they own a territory by loudly slapping their head down on the water or snapping their jaws on its surface. If an intruder approaches, alligators make low growling and hissing noises. They often puff up their bodies and rise up in the water, to appear as big as possible. Fights are fairly rare as the biggest, noisiest animal usually wins. However, if two alligators are of similar size they crash their heads together and try to bite, often locking jaws. Fights are usually short and the injuries are not fatal.

Male alligators chase away other males from the females in their territory that they hope to mate with.

Attracting a mate

Male American alligators attract females by bellowing. They usually bellow from open stretches of water, where they can be heard from all around. The male arches his head and tail out of the water, sucks in air, puffs out his throat and blows the air out in short, deep-toned bellows. The deepest rumble noises can be heard by other alligators several kilometres away. Other males in the area often also start bellowing, in competition. This can last for up to 30 minutes.

Courtship and nesting

Once a female has chosen her male, he starts a **courtship** display. This involves movements or behaviours that tell her he wants to **mate**. For example, he rubs her head and back with his chin, and blows bubbles past her. The pair stay together a few days before they mate under water. The male then leaves, and takes no further part in breeding.

The female finds a sheltered spot near water. She builds a nest out of rooted-up plants, dead sticks and leaves, and mud. She then digs into the nest, lays her eggs and covers them with dead plants. As these plants rot, they produce heat that **incubates** the eggs. The nest is always built above water level, as the developing **embryos** inside the eggs breathe through the shells and would drown under water.

Alligator facts

American alligators can lay 20–80 eggs, but usually around 30.

Their eggs are white, hard-skinned and around 7–9 centimetres long.

The eggs take 65 days to incubate.

This alligator's nest is sheltered amongst trees. The eggs have been uncovered so we can see them.

Young alligators

The eggs and young of American alligators are threatened by **predators**. Until they have grown to over 1.5 metres, their life can be very dangerous.

Female American alligators spend a lot of time near or on their nests, guarding the eggs from predators such as racoons and skunks. When the young alligators are ready to hatch, usually in August, they make a high-pitched croaking noise. This is to tell each other it is time to hatch, and to tell their mother they are coming out into the open, where they may be in danger. To break open the hard egg, the babies slice into the tough skin inside using an egg tooth. This is actually a special sharp **scale** on the tip of their upper jaw. They then push their jaws out of the hole to crack the outer shell.

Baby alligators in a brood hatch from their eggs within a few hours of each other.

When they are fully or partially hatched the young alligators grunt, to tell the mother to chew and claw open the nest that has hardened in the Sun. Without her help, the babies may be trapped. If any eggs have not hatched properly, she may pick them up in her jaws and gently use her tongue to break them.

The babies make for the safety of the water nearest the nest. The female sometimes carries them in her mouth, up to ten at one time. Once in the water, she opens her jaws and moves her head gently from side to side, to wash the babies out.

Pods of baby alligators stay close together for safety in the first six months.

Making contact

Baby alligators and their mother call out to each other to keep in touch. As they get older, these grunting calls are most frequent when they split up to hunt at night, and when they reunite in the morning. If a baby's contact call turns into a chirping distress call, the mother rapidly comes to its aid.

Protection in numbers

Newly hatched baby alligators are around 22 centimetres long, and look just like their parents. They have yellow bands around their bodies to **camouflage** them in the shadowy, weedy water close to the nest. At first, they swim weakly, have soft **scutes** and may be hunted by herons, bullfrogs, some fish and other alligators. The baby alligators form groups called pods. Some babies look out for dangers that might affect them all.

Growing up

In the first years of life, in warm conditions, baby alligators grow up to 30 centimetres a year. Young alligators remain close to their mother, usually for two years. However, she cannot protect them completely from predators. In only two out of every ten alligator eggs laid will the young survive to reach two years. When it is big enough, a young alligator usually leaves its mother to establish its own **home range**.

Adult American alligators do not seem to be vulnerable. They are strong, armoured, good at hunting and have no wild **predators**. However, they do face many dangers, because of the most influential **species** on the planet: humans.

We do not have the natural strength or weapons to defeat alligators. But we have developed behaviour and tools that could kill every alligator and destroy every piece of their **habitat** on Earth.

Population change

When American alligators first walked the Earth, there were no people. About 400 years ago, in 1600, there were around a million **Native Americans** living in tribes all over the USA. Very few of them lived near alligators, because it was dangerous.

The population is growing faster in some US states than in others. Florida's population has grown fast, from 2 million in 1940 to 15 million in 2000.

After the first European **settlers** arrived, the American population began to increase rapidly. Most of these new Americans lived in north-eastern and north-central USA. As the population expanded further, some areas became crowded and settlers moved into new areas further south. Dry areas in the **South** provided the ideal conditions to grow crops such as cotton and oranges.

Problems began when the population here increased. More farmers wanted to grow more crops, and more people wanted places to live. Good farming and housing land is expensive and often in short supply, so bigger areas of **wetland** were drained.

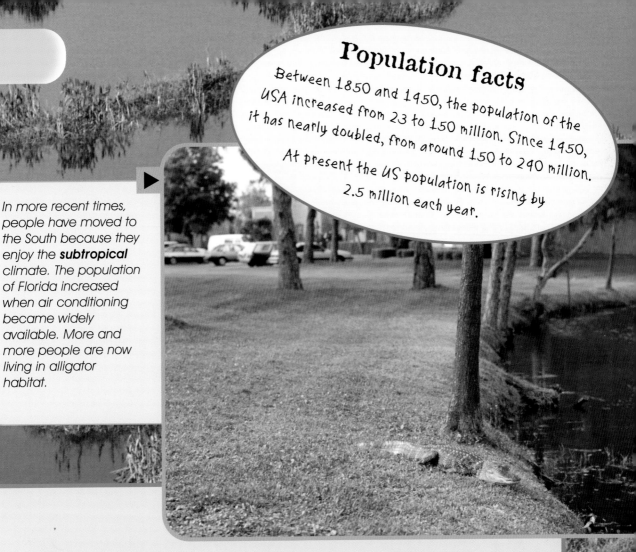

Population facts

Between 1850 and 1950, the population of the USA increased from 23 to 150 million. Since 1950, it has nearly doubled, from around 150 to 240 million. At present the US population is rising by 2.5 million each year.

*In more recent times, people have moved to the South because they enjoy the **subtropical** climate. The population of Florida increased when air conditioning became widely available. More and more people are now living in alligator habitat.*

Competition

As the human population goes up, the population of many wild animals goes down. This is mostly because of competition for natural resources – things animals need to live, including space and food. When more people moved into wetland habitat, they came face to face with American alligators.

At first alligators were killed because it was thought they were a possible threat to people's lives. People were likely to come across alligators when they moved through dense **swamp**, hunting for food such as fish and **wildfowl**. It was also believed that alligators were competing for food people wanted to catch themselves.

Indirect effects of draining wetlands

When people drain wetlands they do not always dry them up. But the draining can change the way the water moves, and the amount of vegetation. This affects alligator populations indirectly. Males need open channels to call females, and females need sheltered spaces in which to build nests. These can both be destroyed by draining.

23

▲ *The meat of the alligator is prized today partly because it is low in fat and high in protein.*

People hunted alligators in small numbers when they first moved into **wetland habitats**. In the 19th century, however, people began to kill many more American alligators, using guns. This was mainly because alligator skin and meat became popular.

Before the middle of the 19th century, alligator skin was just taken off the animal and dried, before being used. It cracked and split fairly easily. After tanning became more easily available, the skin was used more widely. Tanning is a process that makes animal skin more supple and long-lasting. During the American Civil War 1861–65, many soldiers' boots and saddles were made of alligator leather. Oil made from alligator fat was used to lubricate steam engines and machines for spinning cotton. Alligator meat became an important ingredient in regional dishes in the **South** such as gumbo (thick soup). However, most alligators were killed only for use locally or in the region.

Seminole hunters

Some of the earliest **settlers** in the Florida **Everglades** were Seminole Native Americans. They moved into this inhospitable, mosquito-infested land because they were forced off traditional lands further north, during wars with US settlers. The Seminole people became very skilled at hunting and catching alligators. They used all parts of the alligators they killed, from bones for knife handles to teeth for jewellery. Later settlers in the **swamps** used Seminole people as guides, to help them hunt successfully.

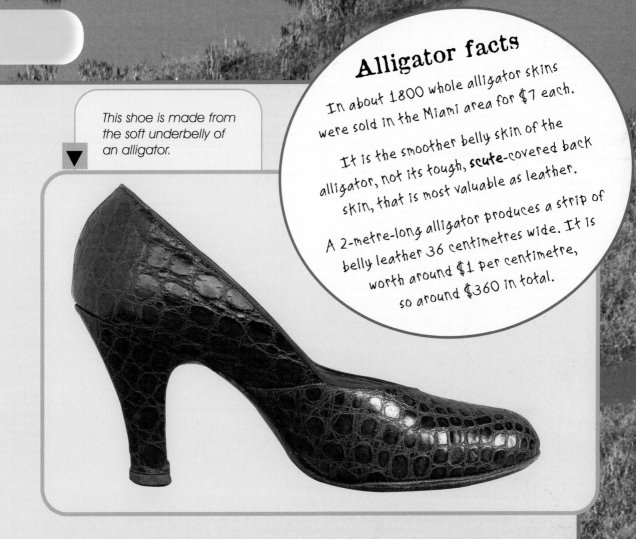

This shoe is made from the soft underbelly of an alligator.

Alligator facts

In about 1800 whole alligator skins were sold in the Miami area for $7 each.

It is the smoother belly skin of the alligator, not its tough, **scute**-covered back skin, that is most valuable as leather.

A 2-metre-long alligator produces a strip of belly leather 36 centimetres wide. It is worth around $1 per centimetre, so around $360 in total.

In the later 19th century, alligator skin became fashionable in Paris, which was then the fashion capital of the world. Many people wanted to wear alligator skin, so they would look fashionable. This meant that it could be sold in large amounts worldwide. It is estimated that between 1850 and 1940 the American alligator population fell by about 10 million as a result.

Decline

During the 20th century, hunters had to catch smaller alligators than before to supply enough skins and to make their living. This meant that more animals were being killed before they reached the size and age when they could **breed**. The Florida state government slowed down hunting in the 1940s and 1950s, by making it illegal to catch small alligators. However, population surveys suggested that the killing was not slowing down enough. This was because many people continued to **poach** during the 1950s and 1960s. By the late 1960s, many scientists believed that alligators were in serious trouble.

Dealing with hunting

In 1967, scientists in the USA stated that the American alligator was an **endangered species**. This meant it was considered in danger of **extinction** in all or a significant part of its **habitat**. In 1969, the US government decided to stop the decline in American alligators.

UNLAWFUL
TO FEED OR HARASS
THESE ALLIGATORS

▲ *Making and enforcing laws has helped protect American alligators.*

Changing the law

The US government first changed a law. It was a law that had stood since 1900, called the Lacey Act. The Lacey Act outlawed trade between states of illegally-killed game. It meant that people could not legally sell the wild animals they had trapped or killed. If they could not sell them, they would not bother to kill them. In 1900 the Lacey Act covered just birds and **mammals**. In 1969, the Endangered Species Conservation Act was formed to include **reptiles**, **amphibians** and fish.

Changing a law is one thing, but enforcing it is another. The US government's Fish and Wildlife Service worked closely with state wildlife and law enforcement agencies. Together they made sure there were enough **conservation** officers to patrol the wild places where alligators live. Good equipment and communication were essential. **Wardens** who are well equipped with boats, binoculars and portable phones can more effectively track **poachers** and work with the police.

This gruesome alligator souvenir was confiscated by customs officers in Germany.

Changing problems

The change in the law stopped hunting outright in the USA. But the Endangered Species Act contained nothing about the trade in skins, either between US states or between countries. The Act was again updated, this time to outlaw the shipment of skins of alligators that had been poached. State and national **customs** officers worked with police and coastguard forces, at borders and around coasts, to stop this **smuggling**. Although some poaching continues today, it is a tiny fraction of the amount in the 1960s and 1970s.

Success story

The Endangered Species Act allowed American alligators to increase in numbers in many areas where populations had become very low. As the alligator began to make a comeback, states where alligators live established programmes to monitor their numbers. This information was used to make sure alligator numbers continued to increase. In 1987, the Fish and Wildlife Service stated that the American alligator was fully recovered, and as a result removed the animal from the list of endangered species.

Continuing hunting

Some alligator hunting did happen in the 1970s and 1980s. The government was reluctant to stop all alligator killing, because the legal trade in alligator skins created many jobs in the **South**. In Louisiana, no alligators were hunted between the early 1960s and 1972. In 1972, hunting was allowed in a small area for a short time. Ten years later, there was a controlled hunting season across the state. In South Carolina, where populations of alligators were much lower, hunting only began again in 1995.

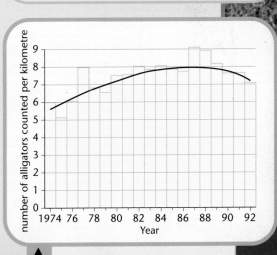

Alligator populations grew from the 1970s to the 1990s.

27

Wild harvesting

The licensed killing of American alligators is called **harvesting**. One type of harvesting is hunting wild alligators. This wild harvesting is controlled, to make sure the population of wild alligators does not decrease.

Managing wild harvesting

The governments of US states carefully manage wild harvests in several ways. Alligator hunts only take place during September. This is when most **breeding** females are near their nests and young. Males are usually in the open water channels where hunters operate. The theory is that as one male generally breeds with several females, removing more males than females means that lots of eggs will still be laid, to keep the population stable.

Each hunter needs a licence issued by the state. First, state scientists decide how many alligators can be killed. In Florida, the results of population counts between years have shown that up to 13 per cent of adult animals can be safely harvested from the population in one year, without affecting the total population in the next year. Then the state decides how many alligators over a certain size can be killed by each licence holder. In Florida in 1999, hunters were allowed to kill five alligators over 1.2 metres long. They were given five tags, one to be put through the tail of each dead alligator.

This Florida trapper is filling out a licence form so he can harvest alligators legally.

The alligators must be hunted in a particular area, where they are plentiful. In this way, areas with fewer alligators are left alone to build up populations. Licences also specify a particular location within the overall hunting area, so hunters do not all go to the same spots.

Wild harvesting methods

Alligators are usually caught with a hook and line. Hunters position strong lines with baited hooks above the water. The height above water is important. If the bait is higher, they are more likely to catch big alligators.

This random method is unlike traditional hunting, where hunters would either shoot or use hooked poles to select the biggest alligators. Bigger alligators produce bigger skins, which can then be sold for more money. However, this often meant that more large females were taken, directly affecting how many eggs were laid each year.

Wild harvesting as conservation

Louisiana **wetlands** are mostly owned by private landowners. Part of each hunter's licence fee goes to the landowner whose land they want to harvest on. As landowners want to preserve this income, they are more likely to look after their areas of wetland **habitat**, and to help stop **poachers**.

Wild harvest facts

A licence costs between $250 and $1000.

Each year, there are around 7000 requests for every 500 licences.

In Louisiana, the state with most alligators, 28–35,000 alligators can be harvested each September.

Hunters are not allowed to put back an alligator they do not want, in the hope of catching a bigger one.

Alligator farms and ranches

The harvest of American alligators from the wild is a small part of the total number **harvested**. Nearly three-quarters of all alligators that are harvested come from farms and ranches. Alligator farms keep adult alligators for **breeding**. These produce young that are reared to become adults. Ranches also raise adults from eggs, but they have no breeding adults to produce the eggs. The adults in both cases are killed and sold as skin and meat.

The right conditions

Alligators need different conditions at different stages in their life. Breeding adults on a farm need a pen large enough to stop the males fighting. There must be deep pools where males and females can **mate**. They must be outside, as seasonal changes in the temperature trigger their **courtship**. There must be plants for shade and for making nest mounds. Breeding alligators should not be disturbed, as any stress may stop them producing young successfully.

Farm facts

There are over 200 alligator farms in the USA, mostly in Louisiana.

It takes 18 months for a hatchling to become a 1.5-metre-long adult on a farm, but 4–5 years in the wild.

Babies grow up to 7.5 centimetres per month on a farm, at a constant temperature of 30 °C.

Between 1972 and 2000, farming and ranching produced 1.7 million skins, worth around $150 million. That is nearly 2000 kilometres of leather!

On farms and ranches alligators are kept in pens with others of the same size and age.

Once the eggs are laid, they are removed from the nests and **incubated** artificially. The temperature is controlled to make sure as many eggs hatch as possible. The temperature is also controlled as the young alligators grow into adults. If it is too cold they will grow more slowly, so it will take longer before they can be sold to make money.

It is expensive to rear alligators. They need lots of space and large pens. For example, each 2-metre-long alligator needs a minimum of 4 square metres. Pens have to be insulated and heated using underground hot water pipes. Alligators also need lots of food, so there needs to be places, like freezers, to store it. They eat anything from waste meat from **slaughterhouses** to special, vitamin-enriched alligator meal.

Ranches

Ranches buy in young alligators from farms or, more usually, collect eggs from the wild. Just like individual alligator hunters, ranches have to pay for a licence to harvest eggs. The state authorities authorize them to take a certain number of eggs, from nests in particular areas. In Louisiana, around 300,000 eggs are taken each year.

Ranches and farms return to the wild up to a sixth of all alligators raised each year, to make up for the eggs they remove.

Destroying American alligator habitat

The **wetlands** where wild American alligators live are being destroyed. **Habitats** are destroyed not only when trees are cut down and water channels filled in or diverted. They can also be destroyed by **pollution**, such as waste chemicals from farms and factories and **sewage** from homes.

Drainage as development

In the past, most people (except a handful of naturalists) considered wetlands a great nuisance. For example, they were home to mosquitoes that spread diseases like malaria. By draining wetlands, engineers removed the still pools where mosquitoes breed and dried up the land. They also diverted the water, through **irrigation** canals, to drier land near by. Between 1870 and 1971, about 5 million acres of wetlands in Florida were destroyed. Today, draining wetlands is rarely considered a way of improving or developing land.

The importance of wetlands

Wetlands form in low-lying places, such as coasts, where groundwater (water held in soil or rock), river water or seawater keeps the ground wet for most of the time. When excess water arrives on land – for example, as rain storms or wind-driven sea waves – wetlands absorb it like a sponge, limiting the effects of flooding. The plants in wetlands also act as a natural filter for material carried by the water such as soil and **nutrients**. Wetlands, then, are important sources of clean water for people, and also stop the **erosion** of land.

When this road was built in the **Everglades**, Florida, it changed the natural water flow and affected the movement of many animals, such as alligators.

There are fewer alligators in water that has been polluted. This scientist is checking water quality.

A rich ecosystem

Wetlands are home to a wide variety of wildlife, as well as alligators. Wetland plants filter out, break down and recycle nutrients that other water plants and animals need. These, in turn, provide food for a rich mixture of **wildfowl**, **amphibians**, **reptiles**, insects and other animals. More than a third of all **endangered species** in the USA live in wetlands, for example the wood stork and the manatee.

The cycle of flooding and drying is also important for wetland wildlife. For example, seeds of the swamp cypress plant can only germinate when the ground dries out. When drainage channels are used to divert water, American alligators can less easily predict which areas will flood. They may build their nests on land that is suddenly flooded, and the eggs inside are lost.

Pollution and the alligator population

During the early 1980s, the alligator population in Lake Apopka, Florida, fell from several thousand to a few hundred. Scientists discovered that fewer eggs were hatching and that babies that did hatch had abnormal sexual **organs**. The abnormalities meant that most alligators in the lake could not breed successfully.

The cause was pollution, by **pesticides** that washed off farmers' fields. Louis Guillette, an alligator biologist, said, 'Lake Apopka leads us to ask some hard questions. What are we doing to the animals around us, and what are the consequences to ourselves?'

Saving American alligator habitat

People save **wetlands** in many practical ways. They set up **reserves** and refuges, or protected areas. They use **wardens** and laws to prevent people developing the land or harming the wildlife there. People also restore spoilt wetlands, by clearing up **pollution** and changing water flow back to how it once was.

However, one of the most important ways of saving wetlands is through education. If people are aware of the importance of wetlands and the value of their wildlife, they will become involved in looking after them.

Money can be raised to help conserve alligators by allowing tourists to view them from a safe distance.

Funding reserves

Most wildlife reserves face the same problem. Reserves exist to create places where animals can live in safety and peace. However, reserves also need visitors, from tourists to licensed hunters, because their money helps to run and maintain the reserves. It costs a lot to employ and equip park rangers, and to look after reserve boundaries.

Animals, such as American alligators, are a great attraction. When alligator **harvesters** pay licence fees to take adults or eggs, some of the money goes towards conservation by private landowners or by reserves and refuges.

When tourists visit alligators in the wild, they pay for tickets, guides and souvenirs. They can also learn more about the rich web of life in the wetlands. Unfortunately, visitors also bring problems, such as more waste and sewage, and noise that disturbs the wildlife.

Restoring the Everglades

In 1948, the US Congress authorized the Central and Southern Florida Project. This water management project aimed to stop flooding, by building canals and dams, and make sure that people living along the south-east coast of the USA near the **Everglades** had enough water throughout the year. Today, the demand for water from the increased population in Florida is much greater, yet the Everglades that supplies so much of its water is around half its original size. What is more, the Everglades are getting drier. They are losing 7 billion litres of fresh water every day, into the Atlantic Ocean and Gulf of Mexico.

Over time the Everglades wildlife has suffered. Many plants are becoming rarer. They are being crowded out by plants that grow particularly well on the phosphorus-rich water that is the result of pollution from farming. When these plants die and rot, they use up oxygen in the water, so animals and fish become more scarce. This means there is less **prey** for other animals.

In 2000, after a thorough study by national, state and local scientists, the US Congress authorized a new 30-year, $8 billion restoration project. It aims to restore some of the original freshwater flow in the Everglades, by removing some canals and dams, widening some natural water channels, building more reservoirs to store water, and clearing up water pollution.

▲ *Large areas of the Everglades are being restored to the wild **habitat** they once were.*

Nuisance alligators

More and more people live in and around **wetlands** in southern USA. Many of them like to live by water. Some go fishing and mess around in boats. Others want to play golf, or swim in their own pool. However, wherever there is suitable water there may be alligators too, and some are a nuisance.

What is a nuisance alligator?

If people choose to live in or near alligator **habitat**, they are likely to encounter alligators. If an alligator lives in a **swamp** by someone's garden, it is not necessarily a nuisance. Nuisance alligators are individuals that are especially aggressive to people, their pets or **livestock**. They are also alligators that hang around near people seeking food, or persistently turn up in places they should not, such as swimming pools, lakes on golf courses, shady places in garages or under cars, and busy town streets.

How do alligators create nuisance?

Some alligators become a nuisance because of the way people behave towards them. Some people go up too close to alligators, or even try to touch them, especially still, **basking** animals. Others throw things at alligators and taunt them. Alligators are then more likely to be aggressive. Some people encourage alligators to come closer by offering them food.

If people feed wild alligators, the animals will associate people with food and are more likely to become a nuisance.

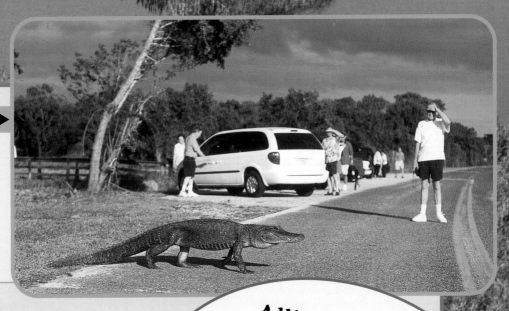

Most alligators that live near people are not a nuisance, so long as they are left well alone.

Alligator attacks

American alligators are large, dangerous **predators**. They do not usually attack people, because they are frightened, but attacks on humans occasionally happen. Alligators may attack young or old people with slower reactions than healthy adults, or they may attack pets. They usually **ambush** from under water, often at dusk. Between 1948 and 1995, there were 218 recorded alligator attacks in Florida. Seven of those attacked died from their injuries.

Alligator facts

Florida's human population, currently 12.5 million, is increasing by over 900 every day. Between 12,000 and 14,000 nuisance alligators are reported in Florida each year. Of these, about 5000 are captured and killed by specially licensed trappers.

Dealing with nuisance alligators

All states in the USA where alligators live have programmes to deal with nuisance alligators. Once an alligator is reported, **conservation** officers visit the area to confirm whether it really is a nuisance. Alligators that have attacked people are shot dead. Specially trained trappers catch the less dangerous nuisances. Some trapped animals are transported and released in different areas of alligator habitat, but they often return to their **home range** within a few days. Persistent nuisance alligators may be sold to an alligator farm. The money this makes goes to the nuisance alligator programme.

The best way to stop alligators harming people is by improving education. Nuisance alligator programme officers visit schools and colleges. They teach students about alligator behaviour, and the importance of respecting and keeping a distance from these animals.

Conservation efforts

There are millions of American alligators in the USA, and in some areas they are very common. Yet this **species** is still described as **threatened**. This means they will become **endangered** if trade in them is not closely monitored. In the USA, laws already monitor trade in American alligator skins and meat. So why call them threatened?

The main reason is to help other crocodilians. There is still much illegal international trade in the skins of endangered crocodilians. Recently, bags and clothes made from their beautiful skins have become fashionable. **Smugglers** hide the skins of crocodiles that have been hunted illegally among legally produced American alligator skins.

American crocodiles are very rare – fewer than a thousand live in the USA.

CITES and crocodilians

CITES (pronounced 'sight-ease') is the short name for the Convention on International Trade in Endangered Species of Wild Fauna and Flora. It was set up in 1975 by 80 countries, to control and regulate international trade in rare species to stop them becoming **extinct**.

Appendix I species are endangered, so threatened with extinction that any trade in them is illegal. Appendix II species are threatened, and they may become endangered or extinct if their trade is not closely monitored. American alligators are registered in Appendix I, even though it is unlikely that they would quickly become endangered if unmonitored.

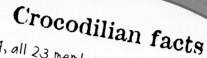

Crocodilian facts

In 1969, all 23 members of the crocodilian **order** were Appendix I. Today only half of them are.

The most critically endangered crocodilians are the Chinese alligator and the Orinoco, Siamese and Philippine crocodiles.

In 2001, a Malaysian reptile smuggler was sentenced to 71 months in prison and fined $60,000 for illegally trading endangered reptiles, including Chinese alligators.

Conservation organizations raise public awareness of endangered crocodilians, caimans and alligators. Their fundraising and scientific expertise is vital to conserving all rare crocodilians.

Stopping smuggling

Police and **customs** authorities work with specialist crocodilian scientists from **conservation** organizations, such as TRAFFIC and WWF, to stop smuggling. Every legally produced American alligator skin is labelled, so any unlabelled skins can be spotted more easily. However, not all crocodilian skins are so carefully labelled. Sometimes the only way to distinguish an endangered crocodilian skin from a more common one that looks similar is by **DNA testing**. Any endangered crocodilian skins are seized by authorities and either destroyed or sold, through legal farms, to raise money for conservation. If smugglers are caught they face fines and prison.

For many poor people, the money from killing and selling a rare wild crocodilian skin is far more than they would normally earn. CITES is working with farmers in crocodilian **habitats** around the world, to set up **harvesting** schemes. In this way, the skins of around a third of all crocodilian species can come from approved ranches and farms, not from wild populations.

Many people think that the revival of American alligator populations in the wild is one of the greatest **conservation** successes of the 20th century.

The success can be divided into three parts. The first is the control of trade in alligators, using laws and licences. This was the result of close co-operation between US national and state governments, CITES, **customs** and police forces, and many scientists and conservation workers. The second part of the success is meeting demand for skins and meat through legal **harvesting**, and not through illegal hunting. The final part is changing the alligator's image. An animal that was once seen as a dangerous nuisance in the **swamps** is now valued, as it can be sold. As alligators now have a value, people are more likely to look after them and improve the **wetlands**.

American alligators link market and marsh. When people buy skins and meat (the market), they help alligators and the marshes where they live.

Supply and demand

Many people argue that one of the best ways to help alligators is to buy and sell alligator products. The problem is that in the US there are more skins being produced by farms than ever before, and not enough customers for alligator products. This means prices are low, and there is less demand for hunted skins. When fewer people hunt and farm, less licence-fee money goes to conservation.

Alligators have been saved from extinction for now, but humans will always be a threat.

Future problems

The future for alligators looks good, but they still face one main problem: **habitat** destruction resulting from the growing human population. This can be slowed down by making sure laws against it are enforced. However, bigger changes may come through educating people about the importance of wetlands in, for example, keeping a good water supply and preventing extreme flooding.

Habitat monitor

Alligators can live for 30, 40 or 50 years, even in fairly **polluted** waters, and their bodies accumulate a record of what they have eaten. This means the alligator is a good monitor of wetland water quality.

There are also newer threats to wetland habitats, such as **climate change**. Over time, changes in weather patterns are creating longer **drought** spells in southern USA, which can dry up wetlands.

Endnote

Some scientists say alligators may never have been **endangered** at all, and that counts in the 1940s to 1960s were inaccurate – alligators were just keeping out of sight of population scientists. This means that even before they were protected, and after a century of intense hunting, alligators were still coping in the wild. Perhaps this can give us hope for the continued success of these remarkable creatures.

How can you help?

Some of the problems facing American alligators and other crocodilians can seem impossible to solve. It is difficult to imagine that as individuals we can make a difference. However, there are many ways in which we can all have a positive impact on the future of these magnificent animals.

Learn more

The first step is to learn more about alligators and other crocodilians by reading books, watching TV programmes, looking at sites on the Internet and visiting them in zoos or alligator farms. You could learn about alligators and crocodiles as part of a class project. Once you are sure of your facts, you can share your knowledge with others and influence how they think.

Speak your mind

One of the best ways to influence the people who make decisions about **wetlands** and alligator **conservation**, such as US state governments, is to tell them how you feel. You could write a letter, or better still start a petition – a letter or statement that lots of people sign to say they agree with it. Different conservation organizations can help you do this. The National Wildlife Federation in the USA, for example, can give details about what to say and where to send your letters. They also publish a number of e-cards on their website, highlighting different **endangered species** in the USA. You can send these by email.

▲ One of the ways you could help in the conservation of alligators is by writing letters to a conservation organization.

Getting close to alligators in a controlled situation is a great way of learning more about them.

You can also speak your mind by becoming active in a conservation group like WWF. You could join a peaceful protest against the destruction of a particular area of wetland. You could help make money for conservation, by taking part in a sponsored walk.

Consumer power

As we have seen, alligator **harvesting** and farming helps to conserve wetlands in the USA. However, if you see any crocodilian products in shops, check to see that they come from a **sustainable** source. This is especially important in some foreign countries where trade in rare crocodilians may not be so carefully monitored.

You can help alligators and other wetland wildlife in your shopping. US conservation groups are urging people to use honey, not sugar, to sweeten their food. This is because growing sugar cane uses a lot of water and **pesticides**. It dries up the land and **pollutes** the water that is left, destroying the **habitat** for wildlife. If people buy locally produced honey, they reduce demand for sugar and so less water is taken from places like the **Everglades**. In Florida, people can pay extra for a car licence plate decorated with a picture of an endangered animal such as a sea turtle or Florida panther. This extra money is spent on the conservation of many different animals in Florida, including alligators.

Glossary

ambush   surprise attack from hiding

amphibians   animals, such as frogs, that start life in water and change as they grow up to live on land

apex predator   animal that eats other animals and is so big or strong that usually no other animals kill or eat it

aquatic   living in water

basking   lying in the sun to get warm

bedrock   solid rock beneath soil or water

breeding   having young, from finding another animal to mate with, to bringing up young

breeding season   time of year when an animal usually breeds

camouflage   colouring or pattern of an animal that helps it blend in with its surroundings

climate   general pattern of weather over a period of years

climate change   change in climate resulting from changes in the Earth's atmosphere

cold-blooded   animal whose body temperature changes with that of its surroundings

conservation   what people do to protect wildlife and the natural habitats of the world

courtship   pattern of behaviour that takes place before mating

customs   government department responsible for controlling the import and export of goods

descendant   later generation. For example, you are a descendant of your grandparents.

digest   break down food so it can be used by the body

DNA testing   identifying an individual or species using its genes (chemical codes that determine how living things are and what they look like)

drought   prolonged period of dry weather

embryo   unborn or unhatched offspring

endangered   species that has so few members it is in danger of becoming extinct

enzymes chemicals in the body that help life processes such as digestion

erosion wearing away of the Earth's surface, for example by water

estuary wetland between a river and the sea, with a mixture of freshwater and saltwater

Everglades National Park at the southern tip of Florida

extinct when a species has died out and no longer exists

fossil preserved remains of a plant or animal that lived millions of years ago

germinate when a seed starts to grow

gland organ that makes some of the chemicals that an animal's body needs

habitat place in the natural world where a particular organism lives

harvesting legal hunting or killing

home range area within a habitat that an animal usually lives in

incubate keep eggs warm so they will hatch

irrigation watering of land by farmers in order to grow crops

livestock farm animals

mammal warm-blooded animal with hair, which can feed its young with milk from its body

mangrove trees specially adapted to live in mud on the seashore

mate when a male animal fertilizes a female's eggs with his sperm

Native Americans original inhabitants of the USA

nutrients chemicals that plants and animals need in order to live

order a level of classification (coming between class and family) for animals and plants

organ part of an animal's body that has a particular function such as the brain or eye

pesticide chemicals used to kill insects and other crop pests

poach hunt and catch or kill animals illegally

pollution when part of the environment is poisoned or harmed by people's activity

predator   animal that hunts and eats other animals

prey   animal that is hunted and eaten by another animal

reptile   animal with scaly skin that lays its eggs on land

reserve   protected area

retina   thin layer at the back of an eye that reacts to light

scales   flat plates of skin forming an outer covering on reptiles and fish

scute   tough, horny scale

settler   person who moves on to uninhabited land

sewage   waste matter such as faeces

slaughterhouse   factory where animals are killed and processed into meat and other products

smuggle   transport hidden goods illegally

South   southern states of the USA

species   group of living things that are similar and can reproduce together to produce healthy offspring

streamlined   shaped to move smoothly through water or air

subtropical   regions north or south of the equator with hot, wet summers and dry, cold winters

survey route   route that is surveyed many times, for example by counting animals, to monitor changes over time

sustainable   keeping something going without using up natural resources

swamp   type of wetland with many trees

territory   particular area an animal claims as its own and defends from others

threatened   at risk of becoming endangered

warden   person paid to guard a particular area such as a reserve

waterfowl   birds that live on or by wetlands, rivers or the sea such as ducks

wetland   area of land completely or partly covered by water

wild fowl   game birds

Websites

crocodilian.com
This comprehensive site covers most things about crocodilians, from natural history to the history of conservation. It includes recordings of crocodilian calls, pictures and information about particular fundraising campaigns to save rare species.

agrigator.ifas.ufl.edu/gators
This site has a variety of information, including details about harvesting and tips on what to do if you meet an alligator.

www.flmnh.ufl.edu/natsci/herpetology/brittoncrocs/csp_amis.htm and
www.uga.edu/srel/gators.htm
You can find lots about the American alligator on these web sites, including some detailed pictures.

www.flmnh.ufl.edu/natsci/herpetology/crocs/csgconservation.htm
This site lists the crocodilian species, ranks them by how rare they are, and gives information on conservation plans and fundraising campaigns.

Books

Alligators and Crocodiles, Karen Dudley (Raintree Steck-Vaughn, 1998)

Alligator – in the Wild, Patricia Kendell (Hodder Wayland, 2002)

The American Alligator, Dorothy Hinshaw Patent (Houghton-Mifflin, 1994)

Wild World: Alligators and Crocodiles, Karen Dudley (A & C Black, 1999)

Videos

BBC Wildlife Specials: Crocodile – the Smiling Predator, narrated by David Attenborough (BBC Video, 1998)

National Geographic Video – Realm of the Alligator, narrated by Pernell Roberts (Quadrant Video, 2000)

Index

Titles in the *Animals Under Threat* series include:

Hardback   0 431 18892 0

Hardback   0 431 18888 2

Hardback   0 431 18889 0

Hardback   0 431 18893 9

Hardback   0 431 18890 4

Hardback   0 431 18891 2

Find out about the other titles in this series on our website www.heinemann.co.uk/library